THE SENSES

The Sense of Touch

by Mari Schuh

Consultant:
Eric H. Chudler, Ph.D.
Director, Neuroscience for Kids
University of Washington
Seattle, Wash.

BLASTOFF! READERS 4

BELLWETHER MEDIA • MINNEAPOLIS, MN

Note to Librarians, Teachers, and Parents:

Blastoff! Readers are carefully developed by literacy experts and combine standards-based content with developmentally-appropriate text.

Level 1 provides the most support through repetition of high-frequency words, light text, predictable sentence patterns, and strong visual support.

Level 2 offers early readers a bit more challenge through varied simple sentences, increased text load, and less repetition of high frequency words.

Level 3 advances early-fluent readers toward fluency through increased text and concept load, less reliance on visuals, longer sentences, and more literary language.

Level 4 builds reading stamina by providing more text per page, increased use of punctuation, greater variation in sentence patterns, and increasingly challenging vocabulary.

Level 5 encourages children to move from "learning to read" to "reading to learn" by providing even more text, varied writing styles, and less familiar topics.

Whichever book is right for your reader, Blastoff! Readers are the perfect books to build confidence and encourage a love of reading that will last a lifetime!

This edition first published in 2008 by Bellwether Media.

No part of this publication may be reproduced in whole or in part without written permission of the publisher. For information regarding permission, write to Bellwether Media Inc., Attention: Permissions Department, Post Office Box 1C, Minnetonka, MN 55345-9998.

Library of Congress Cataloging-in-Publication Data
Schuh, Mari C., 1975–
   The sense of touch / by Mari Schuh.
      p. cm. — (Blastoff! readers. The senses)
Summary: "Introductory text explains the function and experience of the sense of touch. Intended for grades two through five"—Provided by publisher.
   Includes bibliographical references and index.
   ISBN-13: 978-1-60014-074-7 (hardcover : alk. paper)
   ISBN-10: 1-60014-074-2 (hardcover : alk. paper)
   1. Touch—Juvenile literature. I. Title.

QP451.S38 2008
612.8'8—dc22   2007015605

Contents

Your Sense of Touch

Have you ever petted the soft fur of a dog? Have you felt a very smooth stone from a river? You were using your sense of touch.

Touch is one of your senses.
Your other senses are hearing,
sight, taste, and smell.

Your other senses use a small part of your body. You use your ears to hear. You use your eyes to see.

Your tongue helps you to taste.
You use your nose to smell.

Your sense of touch is different. You sense how things feel with your skin. Your skin is all over your body!

What Touch Tells You

Your sense of touch helps you learn about your surroundings. It lets you know an object's **temperature**. A snowball feels cold in your hand. Bathwater might feel hot when you dip your toe in it.

Your sense of touch tells you if
something is rough or smooth.
Tree bark feels rough. The top of
your desk feels smooth.

Your sense of touch helps keep you safe. Your skin senses **pain**. The pain from touching a hot grill tells you to move your hand away.

fun fact

Your outer layer of skin is waterproof! It covers and protects your body.

Touch tells you a cactus is prickly. Ouch!

Your Skin

How does your sense of touch work? It begins inside your skin.

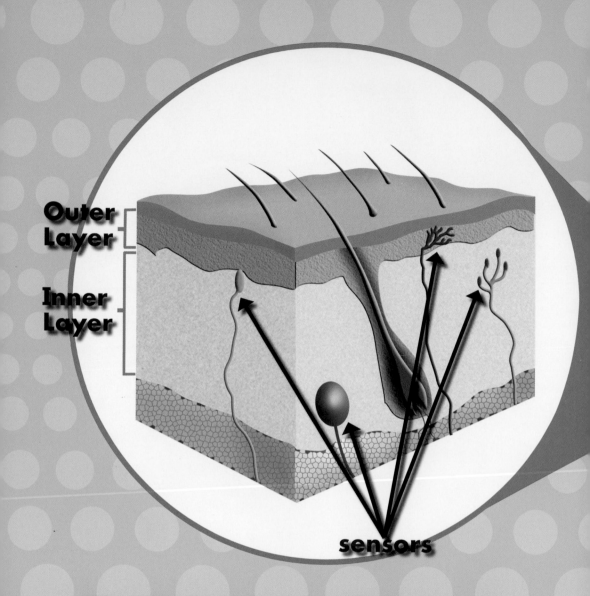

Outer Layer

Inner Layer

sensors

Your skin has two main layers. The thin outer layer has **sensors**. The inner layer of skin is thicker. It has more sensors than the outer layer.

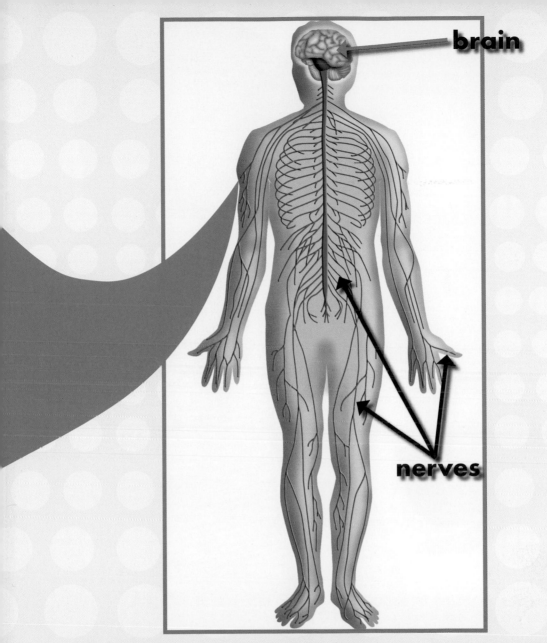

brain

nerves

Sensors connect to **nerves**. These thin threads of tissue run through your body. A nerve carries a message to your brain when a sensor is touched. Your brain tells you about the touch. It all happens in a split second!

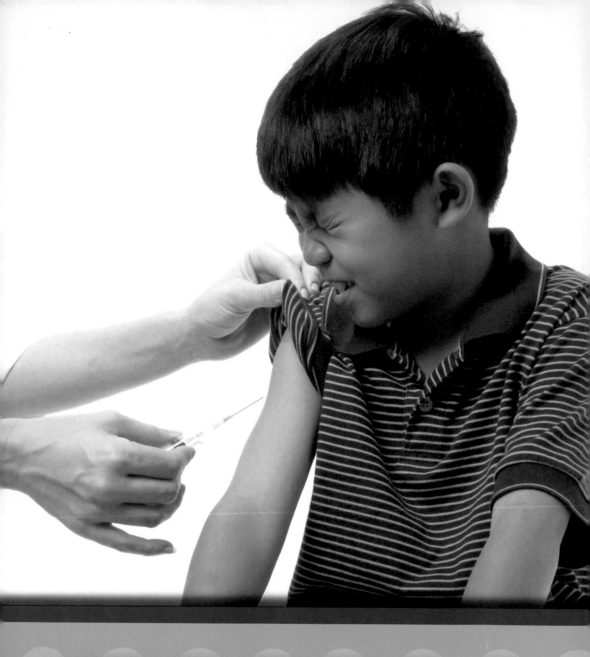

Different sensors have different jobs. Some sensors **detect** pain. Other sensors tell you if something is smooth or rough.

Some sensors know if something is hot or cold.

Touch and Animals

Animals use their sense of touch too. Whiskers help animals like cats and rabbits feel their surroundings. Their whiskers can sense if a space is big enough for them to fit through.

Walruses use their whiskers to search the ocean floor for food. Their whiskers feel for crabs and clams buried in the mud.

fun fact

Skin is your largest organ. It covers your entire body.

Touch Is Important

Your sense of touch is important. It tells you about the world around you and helps keep you safe.

Look around. What kinds of things can you touch? Are they hard or soft? Are they smooth or rough?

Glossary

detect—to notice something is present

nerve—thin strings of tissue throughout your body; nerves carry messages between your brain and other parts of your body.

pain—a feeling of hurt or discomfort

sensors—parts of your body that send messages to your nerves and brain

temperature—the measure of the warmth or coldness of an object

To Learn More

AT THE LIBRARY

Barraclough, Sue. *What Can I Feel?* Chicago, Ill.: Raintree, 2005.

Falk, Laine. *Let's Explore the Five Senses with City Dog and Country Dog.* New York: Children's Press, 2007.

Mackill, Mary. *Touching.* Chicago, Ill.: Heinemann, 2006.

ON THE WEB

Learning more about touch is as easy as 1, 2, 3.

1. Go to www.factsurfer.com

2. Enter "touch" into search box.

3. Click the "Surf" button and you will see a list of related web sites.

With factsurfer.com, finding more information is just a click away.

Index

The images in this book are reproduced through the courtesy of: Hartcreations, front cover; Brian Sytnyk/
Masterfile, p. 4; George Shelley/Masterfile, p. 5; digitalskillet, p. 6; Maribell, p. 7; Anyka, p. 8; Philip &
Karen Smith/Getty Images, p. 9; Elena Elisseeva, p. 10; Ron Chapple/Getty Images, p. 11; Ray Massey/
Getty Images, p. 12; Luc Sesselle, p. 13; Linda Clavel, pp. 14-15; GeoM, p. 16; Brooke Slezak/Getty
Images, p. 17; Elena Sherengovskaya, p. 18; coko, p. 19; Veer Steven Puetzer/Getty Images, pp. 20-21.